# Personal Finance Does Matter

# **Dedication**

I would like to dedicate this to my lovely wife Stephanie, my number one supporter; and to my three beautiful children Arianna, Nathaniel and Niam. You all are my 'why' behind all that I have accomplished and seek to. I am proud to be your father and I cannot wait to see what God has in store for you.

# Acknowledgement

To God be the glory!

In the journey to pursue this book I would like to thank several influential people who helped me along the way. I would first like to thank the Harris', Cory and Gloria for planting the seed of financial stability by facilitating the Dave Ramsey course at our church. I would like to thank my Pastor, Andre Silvers for giving me a platform to spread my roots and grow. Finally, I would like to acknowledge those of you who have supported me by purchasing this book. Let it be forever life changing and inspiring to you.

## Wealth:

What does wealth mean to you? How has wealth impacted the Black community since the inception of this great nation? People perceive what wealth is in many different ways. Some see wealth as assets minus debt, while some measure it with the time they've spent with family and loved ones. Some look at it as having their health, and some may consider having all of what I've mentioned. Webster's Dictionary defines wealth as 'an abundance of valuable material possessions or resources'. In this book, we will take a look at each of these. I believe that no matter what wealth means to you, we will always arrive at the same key points in the end. Wealth is what we all strive for to have and live a better life.

*******

*History of Wealth in the Black Community:*
Growing up we all learned about slavery and the impact it has had on the black community in some way or another. We were taught about the transfer of slaves from Africa to the Caribbean then to the United States. We learned about the Civil war,

how the North fought against the South. We learned about the Emancipation Proclamation declaring the freedom of the slaves. We learned about the Jim Crow south and how leaders like Dr. Martin Luther King, Malcolm X, Huey P. Newton fought for our Civil Rights. We also learned about integration in the school system with Brown vs The Board of Education. I've learned about these events and all these great people but I was never taught about how slavery and racism impacted our financial well-being.

Growing up, I've always heard the saying 40 acres and a mule. I did not really know much about it. From what I knew, this was promised to slaves after the Civil War as a form of reparation. Doing further research, I found out that freed slaves were the ones to negotiate terms of what they wanted minus the mule, that was later added. They would have been awarded 400,000 acres of land if the promised was honored. I sit here now understanding the power that owning land offers. The United States would be a much different place today if the promise to the slaves was not forfeited. With the ownership of land comes wealth, with wealth comes inheritance, with inheritance comes compounding interest.

Albert Einstein once said, "The strongest force in the universe is compound interest. Compound interest is the 'Eighth Wonder of the World'.

He who understands it-earns it; he who doesn't-pays."

This is a very profound statement. We were kings, queens, chiefs, doctors, teachers, and so much more before being taken from Africa. We were torn from our inheritance. We were broken to believe we were less than animals, not equal, and did have wealth. Because we weren't allowed to be paid a wage and given any form of education, much less financial education, we could not invest and have our money compound over time. This, I believe, is one of the main problems to why you do not see as many black people leaving money as an inheritance from generation to generation. I do believe we can break this trend. Hopefully what is learned here can assist in breaking that tendency.

There is a sense of fear, I believe, towards blacks and minorities when they band together for a common cause. No example is more powerful than that of Black Wall Street. Black Wall Street represents a time when a community of prominent black businesses and owners in 1921 were subjected to race riots and burned to the ground in the neighborhood of Tulsa Oklahoma. I believe in the saying "United We Stand; Divided We Fall".

We, as black people have this sense of separation. We should invest in our communities and businesses as an act of unity but we do not. When I ran a small marketing business I saw this in action. The ones who succeeded in this business were Hispanics, Africans, Asians, and Caucasians. African Americans and Blacks did not do as well because of their skeptical nature or just did not want another black person to do better than them. That is called the "crabs in a barrel syndrome".

Obviously, there are many more factors than what I mentioned but this is what I personally went through. We need to realize that we have significant purchasing power in the United States. Black buying power is projected to reach $1.2 trillion in 2017 and $1.4 trillion by 2020, according to a report from the University of Georgia's Selig Center for Economic Growth. That's 275 percent growth since 1990, when black buying power was $320 billion.

<u>Assets</u>

*Assets Minus Debt:*
Assets are defined as items of ownership that are convertible into cash. Debt is defined as items that you currently have to pay off. A couple examples of assets are homes, rental properties, vehicles, savings, stocks, and equipment to name a few. Some examples of debt are student loans, car payments, property, bank loans, and credit cards. When you have more assets than debt you can then

gauge what your wealth is. So, for example, let's take Chris. Chris is a 44-year-old accountant. He owns a home that has a mortgage of $200,000. He has $50,000 of equity in his house. He has a car that he owes $10,000 on. He has student loans that total up to $45,000. He also has a retirement account containing $150,000 and a savings account that holds $20,000. Let's calculate what Chris's total wealth is:

| **Debt** | | **Assets** | | **Net Wealth** |
|---|---|---|---|---|
| **House** | 200,000 | House Equity | 50,000 | |
| **Car** | 10,000 | Retirement | 150,000 | |
| **Student Loan** | 45,000 | Savings | 20,000 | |
| **Total** | **255,000** | - | **220,000** | **-35,000** |

We can see in this example that Chris has a net wealth total of $-35,000. This is what many

Americans are going through. When I look at this chart it doesn't intimidate me because once the house, car, and student loans are paid off, he will be in a great position.

### *Time Spent with Family and Loved Ones*

I come from a very strong family oriented background. It is impossible to assign a monetary value on time spent with family and loved ones. Having those that support you in your presence is one of the best gifts anyone could ask for. When I am on my death bed and I reminisce retrospectively, I won't think about all the money that I made in my lifetime. What will matter is all the lives I've touched along the way, the people I've helped, the lives I've helped create, and the love I've received. To me in the end, that is priceless.

### *Health*

What is having all the money in world but lacking health? If you do not take care of yourself, your time here on this earth will be short lived. I go to the gym every day and when I talk to some of the older members, they tell me that increasing one's longevity is priceless. I have spoken to people in the gym who looked to be in their late 30's but who were actually in their mid-50's. I've also spoken to people outside the gym who looked to be in their late 40's who were actually in their mid-30's. I can see why health and wealth are so similar in spelling, to me they are synonymous.

I am writing this book as a guide to help you achieve your version of wealth. I believe that no matter what your definition of wealth is, there's commonalities with it all. We all are striving to live long, healthy, prosperous lives. I applaud you for taking the first steps in this journey. If you follow this blueprint and create positive habits, I assure you, you will hit all your goals.

### **Let's set some goals:**

The first thing I would like you to do is set some goals. Having goals are important in life. Goals help us look forward to what's to come. Another great thing about goals are, you can track them. You can track your progress. It is important to write them down to see where we were and where we are now. A goal that is not written down is a wish. If your goal is to buy a house in 5 years, write that goal down. Write how much is needed to save as a down payment and then come up with an action plan. To prepare yourself, you might need to obtain a second form of income and read up on the housing market to be more educated on your investment. Research is key and you might need to work with a realtor in the area that will help you meet your goals. All of these should be in your action plan plus whatever else you feel is important. These are the necessary tools to achieve your vision of home ownership.

Having a vision board is also a great way of setting goals. I have a vision board in my office of some of the things I want for my family and myself. This board is a constant reminder that my hard work is a work in progress. I get energized every time I see my vision board and it reminds me that my dreams can become a reality. Some things that I have on my vision board are pictures of vacation locations, my dream house, something representing financial independence and much more. Your vision board should be a reflection of your goals.

Once you have written all of your goals down and created a vision board, you can then create an action plan to achieve them. Your action plan is going to be critical. Your action plan is the steps needed to materialize what is on the vision board. Keep in mind your plan may vary due to unforeseen life events. The next chapter will explain how to use your action plan to bring to pass your vision board. I will explain what I feel you should have in your action plan in the next chapter.

### *Action Plan:*

Let's create an action plan! In order to hit your financial goals, you need to be able to put a check mark on these 10 categories.

Chapter 1) Create a Monthly Budget

Chapter 2) Start Paying Off Debt

Chapter 3) Savings

Chapter 4) Insurance

Chapter 5) Tax Returns

Chapter 6) The American Dream

Chapter 7) Save For Retirement

Chapter 8) Read More

Chapter 9) Look Out

Chapter 10) Pay It Forward

Chapter 11) Closing

# Chapter 1:

# Create A Monthly Budget

Creating a monthly budget is the most important tool you can utilize when starting your journey to financial independence. Roughly only one in three Americans do a monthly budget. That is a very depressing number because if you ask the average person to break down where their money goes every month, they cannot account for it. According to the Census ACS survey (the latest data available), the median household income for the United States was $55,775 in 2015. Your household income may be lower or higher than the average but we all need to know where our money is going. In this chapter, we will break down the most commonly budgeted items so that you can create a monthly budget every month. These items include income, savings, housing, utilities, food, clothing, transportation, personal care, consumer debt, and insurance. Let's take a look at each category separately.

**Income:**

The first thing that I recommend be done is decide what your monthly income is. If you are using your gross and salary this will be easy for you because your base income stays the same. If you are hourly or have income that is not constant, what I would suggest you do is use a month that your income was the lowest and use that number as you're starting point. Doing it this way will set the bar and the average for money earned. It is better to have extra money at the end of the month that wasn't budgeted for than having less money than what was budgeted for. Now, that you have your number we can start assigning it to our categories. You want to make sure that all of your income is assigned to a category. The goal is that when you complete your budget you should have 0 dollars left over because it will all be assigned to a specific category.

**Savings:**

When it comes to the savings category, you want to make sure you **pay yourself first**. You worked hard for your money, so it's only right that you get to keep some of it. You can save for things like an emergency, retirement (if you do not already have money coming out of your check through your employer), college fund (if you have kids), vacation, house, car, or rainy day. So, under your savings category apply sub sections and name them so that you can apply a dollar amount to them.

**Housing:**

Under the housing category you will assign a dollar amount for housing. Depending on whether you own your home or make rental payments you will put what money you spend in each respective category. In this section, if applicable, put special sections of any taxes that you have to pay, any associations fees you have to pay, and/or any lawn care or maintenance fees you have to pay if you reside in a location that gives that luxury.

**Utilities:**

Utilities are any recurring bills you pay monthly that can never be paid off. Some utilities fees that should be in your budget include gas/oil, water, electricity, and cable/internet. Depending on where you live you may have other utilities you can put in your budget. Just remember that these types of bills do not get paid off as they are essential to the upkeep of your home. They are due every month for that reason.

**Food:**

Assigning a food budget is a great way to save money. Eating out costs money and its best to decide how much money is spent weekly and monthly in accordance with your pay period and stick to it. This can change every month but it is important to assign a dollar amount there even if all you buy is a small amount. A restaurant budget will be an eye opener for many of you reading this book. We don't realize how much money we spend eating out. Things that coincide with our restaurant budget number are, if you buy lunch every day at work, the coffee you buy, drinks at a bar, club, or lounge, and dinners at a restaurant. The numbers add up and can seriously make a dent in your saving progress.

**Clothing:**

As humans, we need to wear clothes. With that being said there should be a budget for it especially if you wear uniforms for employment. There's a tax write off for it at the end of the year. Whether it's new clothes that is purchased or dry cleaning or laundry expense it should be factored in.

**Transportation:**

Transportation is a key form of getting from place to place no matter where you are located. Whether you use a car or public transportation or even Uber, it is wise to include a budget for that so we know how much is being spent monthly. It can get costly and if you are driving include possible repair expenses as well.

**Personal Care:**

Personal care items vary and can range from a few different areas. In this category, you will add those that you and your family use every day. Some things to consider would be miscellaneous items such as daycare, petty cash expenses, gifts, toiletries, make-up and hair care, child support, alimony, organizational dues, etc. Whatever you believe is important to you and your family or that personally affects you and your family, will go in this section.

**Consumer Debt:**

Debt is something that you should have in your budget. Assigning a dollar amount to the amount owed will help pay it off and hopefully never go back into it. Debts are things that you can pay off completely without them returning. Your payment history helps your credit score go up as you continue making regular on time payments.

**Insurance:**

Insurance category is very important. Insurance is a tool to be utilized that will protect us and our assets. Things in this category are health insurance (if you pay out of pocket), life insurance, vehicle insurance (car, bike, boat, RV, etc), identity theft, and home or renters insurance to name a few. It is very important that we have insurance that covers all aspects of our lives. At any moment, an emergency can occur to which you or your family could be left in a position that leaves you financially strapped. Insurance protects for those moments.

# Chapter 2:

# Start Paying Off Debt

**L**ets see if this sounds like you. You go to school for 4 years. You accumulate a massive amount of student loan debt. It's hard to find a job in your major so you settle for anything so that you can start paying off your student loans. The job you find is not paying you what you would like but instead of negotiating a starting salary, you're just happy that you have a job. Now that you have a job, probably in the state that your college or university is, you rent an apartment. So here is how life is going for you now: you have a job that's not paying you what you would like, you are living in an apartment that is overpriced with regards to utilities and expenses. You also need to start making payments on your student loans, and you probably have a car payment because you need to be able to get to work, plus buying everyday necessities.

What do we do in order to buy us some time in a scenario like this? We put it on our credit cards and incur a massive amount of debt that we need to pay off. This affects us as we get older. We meet someone, we start having kids, our salary gets better, we have two incomes now but our debt is still lingering in the background. Having debt should not feel common. It should not be something that we have all of our lives. We should want to pay it all off as fast as we can so that we can start building wealth.

The best way that I've learned how to pay off debt is by using a snowball approach. This approach works by listing all of your debt from smallest to largest and then once one is paid off you take the money that you would apply to the one that's paid off and apply it to the next debt. You keep doing this until all your debt is paid off. This approach is like a snowball building up speed going down a hill, and this is a great example as to how you should pay off your debt. Take this graph below as an example.

| Debt | Minimum Payment | Total Amount | New Payment |
|---|---|---|---|
| Card 1 | 50 | 1,000 | |
| Card 2 | 75 | 1,500 | |
| Card 3 | 100 | 2,000 | |
| Car Payment | 479 | 15,000 | |
| Student Loans | 500 | 30,000 | |

| Debt | Minimum Payment | Total Amount | New Payment |
|---|---|---|---|
| Card 1 | 0 | 0 | |
| Card 2 | 75 | 1,500 | 50 + 75 = 125 |
| Card 3 | 100 | 2,000 | |
| Car Payment | 479 | 15,000 | |
| Student Loan | 300 | 30,000 | |

| Debt | Minimum Payment | Total Amount | New Payment |
|---|---|---|---|
| Card 1 | 0 | 0 | |
| Card 2 | 0 | 0 | |
| Card 3 | 100 | 2,000 | 50+75+100 =225 |
| Car Payment | 479 | 15,000 | |
| Student Loan | 300 | 30,000 | |

| Debt | Minimum Payment | Total Amount | New Payment |
|---|---|---|---|
| Card 1 | 0 | 0 | |
| Card 2 | 0 | 0 | |
| Card 3 | 0 | 0 | |
| Car Payment | 479 | 15,000 | 50+75+100+479= 704 |
| Student Loan | 300 | 30,000 | |

| Debt | Minimum Payment | Total Amount | New Payment |
|---|---|---|---|
| Card 1 | 0 | 0 | |
| Card 2 | 0 | 0 | |
| Card 3 | 0 | 0 | |
| Car Payment | 0 | 0 | |
| Student Loan | 300 | 30,000 | 50+75+100+479+300= 1,004 |

The goal is to make your minimum payments while your next debt inline gets extra money thrown at it. This is a very effective way of paying off debt. My wife and I have paid off close to $100,000 in debt using this method. We have paid off 3 vehicles, 8 credit cards, 2 student loans, several medical bills, and a bank loan in less than 3 years using this method. I am not only advising it, I am a living example that it works.

Always think ahead:

One thing that I always lived by is that whatever my current circumstance was, it could always change. I thought, since I have an emergency savings account in place, I should do that for other areas of my life. The main area that I knew I would need an exit plan was work. After graduating college in 2008, during one of the worst economic climates that this country has gone through in a while, I knew that getting a job and holding on to one would be a challenge. Companies at that time were cutting in every area they could to save money.

I was fortunate to find a decent job out of college. During this time, I viewed employees who lost their full-time status and were bumped down to part time thus experiencing a loss of benefits. I saw our company's retirement match program go from 6% to 3%. Any person going through an uncomfortable time like this begins to think of ways to make themselves more employable, due to them not knowing about the future of their job. I decided that I would do just that.

What I chose to do to become more employable was to build my resume. My first step was to go back to school and get my MBA. Once I received my degree, I took on part time jobs in different fields of management to gain experience. Another thing I did was, get as much certifications as possible to validate my knowledge within my industries. Finally, I put my resume out there to see what I would be worth. Now I don't suggest that you apply for jobs that you don't intend to do but what I would do is contact employers with my resume and ask, what would I be worth to your company. Let them know that they'll be helping you out by helping you gauge your worth. Another reason why this method is good is because now you can use this person as a contact and they are now a part of your network.

A huge advantage in getting a part time job is having another revenue stream. Having multiple revenue streams will help you get to your financial goals much sooner than later. In addition, that part time job may turn into something you love doing. This might turn your position from something temporary to permanent and you can be eligible for a promotion. This would elevate you financially as well as laterally with more responsibilities.

Your final option would be to possibly think of different ways to set up a business. Think of things that you do well or have a passion for. You like working out, get a personal trainer certificate and open your own personal training company. You enjoy cooking, open up a small restaurant or bakery shop. Are you good in a certain subject like math, English, or even speak a foreign language, then open up a tutoring business on the side. There are so many different avenues you can go when thinking about opening up a small business.

# Chapter 3:

# Savings

Saving money should be as common as spending but unfortunately it is not. There are several things I believe that we should be saving for. We should be saving for emergencies, purchases, retirement, kids college, and a home. Let's take a look at each of these more closely.

**Emergency Savings:**

I read a recent article that stated that 66 million working Americans do not have any emergency savings. Some may say, "That's what I have a credit card for". Having a credit card is not a form of "Savings" but a form of "Borrowing". A true emergency fund is three to six months of expenses. Once you've completed your monthly budget, that number will be easy to calculate. Another study shows that forty-seven percent of working Americans could not cover an emergency of $400 and would need to borrow (credit cards) or sell something to cover it. Like I mentioned in the chapter on budgeting, you need to pay yourself first.

It's ideal to set up a savings account at a bank or credit union and have money put in there from every check via direct deposit. This is a good way to save because you're not feeling the money go into the account, thus eliminating the attachment. It is best to start off small while you're paying off your debt and then gradually increase. If you're not the best at saving and feel you may spend your savings, choose a credit union or bank where you can separate your accounts so it's not readily accessible. Another idea is to not have any checks or ATM cards associated with the account.

**Retirement:**

I recently read an article that says 68% of working Americans do not contribute to a 401k plan according to Forbes.com. Please do not fall victim to this statistic. I know I do not want to work forever so I need to know what my walk away number is and then come up with an action plan to get there. "Walk away number"; what's that?

Have you ever been to a casino and where you bring in with you a certain amount of money and say to yourself if I flip this $300 into $3000 I will walk away? So, what is the number that you would need to reach to retire like you want to and walk away from work? Once you know that number, you will now be able to set up an action plan in order to get there.

How did I figure out what my number is you might be asking? There are many ways you can do this. You can go to a financial advisor and have them run an analysis for you. You can also go to your banking institute and ask to have a retirement analysis run if they do those as well. Finally, there are sites you can go to on the internet that will help you find that number. One of my favorite sites to use is www.chrishogan360.com. This site is a great tool for retirement. It has helped me a great deal and I'm sure it can do the same for you.

**Saving for Purchases**

We live in an era where we want things instantly. We do not want to wait and buy things anymore. If you want to go on a vacation you put it on a credit card, if you want to buy a car you take out a loan, if you want furniture you finance it. What happened to putting money aside and paying cash for things? It can be done. My wife and I haven't used a credit card in 3 years and we have bought furniture, gone on vacations, and currently saving to upgrade our vehicles.

Do you know what the difference is from a vacation and a trip? Most people think they are taking vacations but they're not, they're taking trips. When you go on vacation, it's supposed to be a time of rest and relaxation. It is not to worry about the massive credit card debt you just went into to get there. That's what you call a trip because you're tripping when the credit card statement comes in the mail.

Saving to buy a nice car is not as hard as you think. Right now, we have a reliable vehicle but we know that we will need another vehicle because our family is growing. We have recently begun a vehicle savings account at one of the local credit unions. We put a set amount in this account weekly. When it is time to upgrade, we will sell our vehicle and add the money from our savings and buy our next vehicle all in cash. You may be thinking, "Well that sounds good but I don't have a current vehicle." I suggest getting an inexpensive car. I find it would be best to get something that is reliable and gets you to and from work. You can use the savings approach we just spoke about and then sell that car, add your savings on top of that and buy something better. Keep doing that until you can buy your dream car in cash with no car payments.

**Kids College Savings**

Student loan debt is at an all-time high. Let's start breaking the cycle of having our children graduate with thousands of dollars in student loan debt.

A recent article from CNBC states that, "In 18 years, the average sticker price for a private university could be as much as $130,428 a year. The situation isn't much better if you go the public route. Sending your child to a state university could set you back at least $41,228 a year." If you have kids it's a good idea to meet with an investment planner and set up a account for your children or set up a **529**.

A **529** is a college savings plan that has a tax-advantaged program designed to help individuals and families save for college. There are important advantages for you including tax-deferred growth and no income limits. In addition, distributions for qualified education expenses are free from federal taxes, and may also be free from state taxes. Make sure the person you ask to help you set this account up can explain it in a way that you can understand. I tell people all the time to explain certain things to me as if I were a child. My goal is to be able to explain it to the next person and have them understand it as well. I would suggest setting this account up once you're out of debt.

For parents with children who are closer to going to college I would suggest a few different options. The first thing you want to do is have your child take the S.A. T's as many times as it takes to get a high score. The higher the score, the more scholarships become available to you. Secondly, apply for as many grants and scholarships as possible. This comes from conferring with counselors and doing research on the best scholarships and grants that would benefit your child. One site that can help is www.myscholly.com. The school should be able to assist in this. Finally, going to a community college is an excellent choice. There you have the option to take all your electives, then go to the college of your choice that will accept all your elective credits. While your child is attending community college, make sure he or she is working and paying for college as they go. It's also a good idea to go to a local college and university because they're significantly cheaper than out of state colleges and universities.

Finally, if you've saved enough money for your child to go to college for free or your child has received a full scholarship, now is the time to encourage employment. There is no rule that states that you cannot work and attend school at the same time. I understand you want them to focus on their education but having them work and save money for after graduation will go a long way. It will help them better understand the value of a dollar. If you have saved money for them, specifically for their education, imagine being able to gift that money to them knowing that they can handle and respect the gift. I worked all through college and grad school and it was a gratifying experience.

**House Savings**

It is not impossible to buy a house outright. It all depends on your level of savings and how good you are at savings. I have heard stories of people saving and buying their first home outright.

If you are going to take out a mortgage, you should put as much down as possible but a minimum of 20% so you do not have to pay Private Mortgage Insurance(PMI). PMI is a special type of insurance policy, provided by private insurers, to protect a lender against loss if a borrower defaults. This payment does not go toward helping you pay down your mortgage. It is basically an insurance policy for the lender not you. It is a waste of money. That's why you should want to put at least 20% down so you won't have to pay this fee. Also, it's best to take out a conventional loan. These loans have quite a few benefits such as less paperwork, quicker loan turn-around times, no PMI because of the 20% down, fixed interest rates, and options to pay taxes separate from your actual mortgage payment making your monthly payments less.

My advice to you is to take out a 15-year mortgage instead of a 30-year mortgage. With a 15-year mortgage, you will pay a few hundred dollars more a month compared to a 30-year mortgage but you will save a lot of money on the interest. Let's take for example you purchase a 200,000 home with a fixed rate of 3.5%, your monthly payments would be around 1,430. You will pay a total of $57,358 in interest for the 15 years on the loan. Now let's take a 30year mortgage. Normally the interest rate is higher on a 30-year compared to a 15-year according to bankrate.com. But in this example, we will keep the same interest rate of 3.5. Your mortgage payments per month would be $898.00 on a 3.5% interest rate which is cheaper than the 15-year but you will pay 123,312 for the life time of the loan. You are paying $65,954 more in interest in a 30-year loan compared to that of a 15 year. I would gladly pay 532 more a month if it will save me $65,954.

See chart below:

| 15 Year Mortgage | | 30 Year Mortgage | | Difference |
|---|---|---|---|---|
| Cost of Home | $200,000 | Cost of Home | 200,000 | |
| Fixed Interest Rate | 3.5 | Fixed Interest Rate | 3.5 | |
| Monthly Payment | $1,430 | Monthly Payment | $898.00 | $532 |
| 15 Years Interest | $57,358 | 30 Years Interest | $123,312 | $65,954 |

# Chapter 4:

# Insurance

Insurance is an important tool for and while building wealth. Having insurance covers you and your valuables in case of damage, loss, or death. In this chapter, I will cover the importance of having life insurance. Unlike car insurance, which is mandatory, life insurance is an option but it is just as if not, more valuable to possess. I know a lot about insurance because I use to be a representative. I will discuss the different types of insurances that I sold. They were Whole Life, Universal life, and Term life insurance.

**Whole Life Insurance:**

Whole life insurance policies are life insurance policies that pay a benefit on the death of the insured throughout the entire life of the policy holder and accumulates a cash value. This policy is the most expensive policy you can take out in relation to other life insurance policies. Insurance agents love selling these policies because they receive the best commissions on them. When I was in insurance and if I sold this policy, I would get the 65% of the first year's premium payment and then 35% in a couple years and then 20% every year that the policy is in good standing. For example, if I wrote a policy for $150 a month, $1,800 a year, I would get a check for $1,170. After a couple years of the policy being in good standings I would receive $630. This is what people in the insurance business call residual income. As long as the policy stays in good standing, you will receive income from the life time of the policy and you only had one meeting with the client. This is why many agents will do whatever it takes to land the sale.

The cash value in an insurance plan is one of the selling points they focus on when introducing a whole life policy. The way the cash value plan works is through investments. When you make your monthly payments, a portion of the payment is invested, the interest on that investment is what builds your cash value. The interest rates aren't good. You could actually make more money investing the money yourself in mutual funds. The biggest catch to this policy that we wouldn't tell our customers is that, if you die, the cash value that has accrued stays with the insurance company. You do not get to keep the money, you only get the value of the policy. So, for example, if you took out a $80,000 dollar Whole Life policy and it accrued $15,000 cash value, your beneficiary would only receive $80,000.

The insurance company I worked for briefly would meet every Monday night and set up our appointments for the week. We only focused on low income families and neighborhoods. I was very uncomfortable with that but I was new so I wanted to see where this would take me. I called a client one day and because of his work schedule he could only meet on Mondays. I told my supervisor that I had an appointment during our office hours and it sounded like a potential sale, so he let me go. This client lived in a decent neighborhood and had a decent job. I went through my spiel, although rather nervous but I sold the account. My first sale, I was extremely excited. Made around $1,100 for an hour and a half of work. I shook the clients hand, went to my car and drove to the next neighborhood; parked and calmed my nerves. Once my adrenaline calmed down and I was back in my right mind, I realized that I sold a policy to a family that could have purchased a term life policy for 4 times less and would have been covered 10 times more. As you could tell, I didn't last much longer and resigned a couple weeks later. My conscience wouldn't allow me to continue.

**Universal Life:**

A Universal Life Insurance policy is a type of US life insurance which combines the benefits of an adjustable premium, adjustable coverage term life insurance, and a savings account. I'm not going to say much about this policy because it's also in my opinion just as bad as a whole life policy. Anytime you see a savings option in a life insurance plan, don't sign up for it. One of the reasons why people sign up for these policies is because they feel like they are killing two birds with one stone but what they are killing is the growth that they would be getting if they made better investments outside insurance.

**Term Life Insurance:**

Term life insurance is the best insurance I believe you can have. Term life insurance is insurance that stays in effect for a specified period or until a certain age of the insured. It pays the face amount of the policy in case the insured dies within the coverage period (term) but pays nothing if he or she outlives it. It is the cheapest form of insurance but pays the most. My wife and I have a $1,000,000, 20-year term life insurance policy. So, if I were to die within the 20 year term, my beneficiary would receive $500,000. My wife would be able to pay off all our debt, put money aside for our children, and invest and spend the rest. This is a great way to leave your family an inheritance instead of debt in a time of grieving.

I have seen cases in which a loved one dies and leaves the beneficiary with nothing but debt and I've seen cases where there's a substantial amount left behind. Can you imagine losing a loved one and inheriting their debt, once the grieving period is over, the financial reality will hit. You have lost an income contributor in the household but still have the debt. You will be a total mess. Not a good scenario but it happens to millions of people. Now Imagine losing a loved one, an income contributor, and having enough money to pay off all debt. After the grieving period, you will be in a much better place. Do yourself a major favor. If you have people who depend on you, get the proper life insurance.

# Chapter 5:

# Tax Returns

There was a debate on tax returns on my Facebook page one day. I've noticed that a lot of people post all the plans they have for their tax returns. Bragging that they're going to be getting a large refund check. I'm going to explain to you why getting a refund check isn't something to celebrate about.

First in order to understand refund checks I think it is a great idea to understand tax brackets. Tax brackets are a range of incomes and the actual percent you pay on those incomes. You can file single, married filing jointly, married filing separately, or head of household. No matter how you choose to file, the percentages stay the same and the amount of income in each percent bracket changes. **Remember, like seasons, these tax brackets can change.** In order to keep on top of them, check in on the IRS website or ask your local tax professional or accountant.

10% $0-9,275
15% $9,276-$37,650
25% $37,651-$91,150
28% $91,151-$190,150
33% $190,151-$413,350
35% $413,351-$415,050
39.6 $415,051 and more

So, let's say you made $75,000 in the full calendar year of 2016. You would be taxed in the 25% tax bracket. Your end of the year tax would be $14,520.85. Now you are probably wondering, 25% of $75,000 is not $14,520.85 but instead $18,750. Well, that is not how taxes work. Let me explain. The $75,000 you made during the year will be taxed in all the brackets that apply. Let's take a look at the graph below. You will see that your income is taxed in every bracket until it reaches the total of $75,000. So, $9,275 is taxed at 10%, $28,374 is taxed at 15%, and $37,349 is taxed at 25%.

| Tax Per-centage | Income Range | $75,000 Income | Total |
|---|---|---|---|
| 10% | $0-9,275 | $9,275 | $927.5 |
| 15% | $9,276-$37,650 | $28,374 | $4,256.1 |
| 25% | $37,651-$91,150 | $37,349 | $9,337.25 |
|  |  |  | $14,520.85 |

Now there's a myth that if you make more money the next year you get taxed in the next tax bracket fully. That's not true, you will get taxed the amount that spills over into the next tax bracket. So, say for instance in 2017 you found a way to increase your income $100,000 only $8,849 will be taxed in the 28% bracket.

| Tax Percentage | Income Range | $100,000 Income | Total |
|---|---|---|---|
| 10% | $0-9,275 | $9,275 | $927.5 |
| 15% | $9,276-$37,650 | $28,374 | $4,256.1 |
| 25% | $37,651-$91,150 | $37,349 | $9,337.25 |
| 28% | $91,151-$190,150 | $8,849 | $2,477.72 |
|  |  |  | $16,998.57 |

So, you made $8,849 more than the previous year, paid $2,477.72 which netted you $6,371.28. I would take those numbers all day. Working more does not mean that the government will take all your money. They may be special circumstances where this may not work out to your benefit but for the vast majority of us, it does.

In knowing this information, hopefully you can gauge how much you need to pay in taxes to minimize the refund you will get at the end of the year. If you go to the IRS website, they provide a calculator that you can put your information in to see how much to have taken out your check for taxes. People who aren't good with money or do not create a written budget monthly, typically wait until the end of the year for their refund check. I was one of these people. I used to say to myself, "this is a forced savings plan." Now that I look back at it, this wasn't the best idea. Getting a refund check at the end of the year is like putting your money in a bank account that you cannot get to for a year and it gains no interest. Why not get the money that you are over paying in taxes in your pay check weekly, bi-weekly, or monthly. You can use this money for many different reasons. You can build an emergency fund. You can save for purchases. You can set the extra money aside and put in a retirement fund. You can pay off debts a lot sooner. With the money that you over pay in taxes in order to get a bigger check at the end of the year, you can take the money now and build a better and more stable financial system for yourself.

# Chapter 6:

# The American Dream

The American Dream is simple in definition. It is the idea that every US citizen should have an equal opportunity to achieve success and prosperity through hard work, determination, and initiative. How does this definition of the American Dream fit in with your ideals of this country? Do you believe that this dream is attainable? I understand that some races must work harder than others to obtain this dream but I myself like a bit of a challenge. Let us not be depressed with the challenges that are ahead of us but embrace it with vigor and tenacity.

The American Dream for me is making sure that I leave a great inheritance to my children and my children's children. Leaving money, land, real estate, investments, and knowledge of how to manage it all is what I am talking about. I would like to leave them these things that weren't afforded to me. It is important that we understand that the things that our ancestors helped to cultivate, civil right leaders helped to fight for, and our parents worked so hard are within our reach and we are able to have with determination and hard work.

I often wonder why minorities owned so few wealth building items like real estate. When you look back at the history of any developing nation, you realize that the ones who owned land are the ones with the real power. If slaves were afforded their forty acres and a mule, African American people would be in a better shape as a whole than we are today. There have been many regulations in American history that has restricted us from buying homes and benefiting from all the advantages that owning a home offers.

The word "redlining" is a word that few African Americans know but many are living through it. Redlining is a discriminatory practice by which banks, insurance companies, etc., refuse or limit loans, mortgages, insurance, etc., within specific geographic areas, especially inner-city neighborhoods. These companies would map out neighborhoods with color codes that would allow realtors to know what areas would be suitable for black families. The color legend is described as, light blue being the best neighborhoods, blue being the still desirable neighborhoods, yellow being declining neighborhoods, and red being hazardous neighborhoods. This method was used for decades and caused a lot of strife in the minority communities.

I read a great article that stated, "As late as 1950's, the National Association of Real Estate Boards' code of ethic warned that "a realtor should never be instrumental in introducing into a neighborhood...any race or nationality, or individuals whose presence will clearly be detrimental to property values." According to "The Case for Reparations" by Ta-Nehisi Coates, another statement that rung true was, "A 1943 brochure specified that such potential undesirables might include madams, bootleggers, gangsters", and "a colored man of means who was giving his children a college education and thought they were entitled to live among whites."

Today we have the Fair Housing Act (FHA) and the Equal Credit Opportunity Act (ECOA) to protect consumers by prohibiting unfair and discriminatory practices. These acts may be set in place to protect us but the residual effects of redlining are still there. According to "The Case for Reparations" by Ta-Nehisi Coates, black families making $100,000 typically live in the kinds of neighborhoods inhabited by white families making $30,000. We still have some catching up to do but I believe we can do it as long as we become good managers of our money.

My mother and I migrated from Jamaica in 1988. She did not have much to her name but she believed that coming to this country would change our circumstances for the best. She did what most foreigners do, she worked 2-3 jobs to support us. My mother was never a woman to shy away from hard work. She used the ample opportunity of jobs as a way to achieve what she wanted for her family. She landed full time work with benefits, sent her kids to college, and ultimately bought a house. If not for hard work and creating opportunity she would not have been prosperous. I have heard jokes all my life about how Jamaicans and Mexicans work so many jobs but to me that shows determination and the active pursuit of the American dream.

I understand that it may be harder for some to gain the same opportunity as others but I believe this builds character and mental toughness. Those who are opportunist I believe, do better than those let opportunities slip by. A person should be able to learn from all the opportunities they go through in life even if it's not successful.

This reminds me of the time I joined a MLM company. MLM stands for Multi-Level Marketing. At that point in my life I was renting an apartment with my girlfriend and our baby girl. I was content with what I had accomplished in life. I was a successful manager at the company I worked for, I graduated college with my MBA, and was renting an apartment. I felt good.

A college buddy of mine called me one day and invited me to a house warming for the new house he had bought. I was going to go but hit traffic and decided to turn back and go home. He then told me the truth, that he wanted me to look at a business opportunity. I told him I would try and see it one day. He was very eager to have me look at this opportunity so he told me he would pick me up and drive me to an event that was being held by some of the top leaders in the business. Now, up until this point I did not know anything about MLM but being the person I was, I was skeptical. Saturday morning came and he called me and told me he was on his way and that I should get ready. I rolled over mulling over in my mind why I didn't want to go and what excuses I should use. No sooner than I figured out a reason, I heard a beep. It was him. I decided to get ready and take the chance to see what it was all about.

We drove to Springfield at a hotel where the event was being held. I looked around the room and saw some very sharply dressed individuals. I turned to my friend and exclaimed, " Why didn't you tell me I needed to dress up" he responded that guests did not need to.

The conference started with a video of some wealthy individuals who told their story. I was impressed by the vacations they took, the wealth they built, the cars they drove, and that they were my color. At this point I was more than interested. The first speaker who spoke about the process was a local success story. The main speaker was someone from the video I watched. I was extremely excited to hear what he had to say. After the conference was done, my friend took me up to meet the presenter. I felt star struck and nervous to be in the presence of a multi-millionaire. I introduced myself and expressed that I was excited to have been invited to the event and that I would join.

After the event, I told my friend that I wanted to sign up that day. I saw the vision and it's so happened that he caught me at a good time because I was getting my bonus check from my main job in a week and would be able to pay the entrance fee. After paying my franchise fee I took off running. If you know about joining a MLM, you know that there are different positions you hit when you drum up a certain amount of business. I hit the first two positions in a month and hit one of the top positions in less than 5 months. I soon surpassed my friend who brought me in and caught up to the person who was our mentor in the business. I handled over 200 business partners in my line and thousands of customers. I traveled to places I had never been before like California, Louisiana, Las Vegas, and North Carolina. I was so impressed with the company that I got my girlfriend at the time and sister involved. My sister would then turn around and beat my record of getting to one of the top positions in the company in less time than I did.

My journey in the company taught me a lot of transferable skills. I learned how to present and I learned various ways to market. I learned how to handle rejection and how to develop an LLC. I learned all the tax breaks that having a LLC is awarded as well. I was taught how to network with people, I was taught how to manage a team of people spread across different states. This MLM company taught me how to run my own business in real time. I knew about accounting and financial processes through my main job as a manager. I knew about profit and loss, about account payable and receivable, credit and debits, expenses, budgets, etc. The most important thing that working at a MLM taught me was that it was ok to dream about being your own boss and letting money work for you.

Ultimately, I stayed with the company for 3 years and when my line started to fall apart I decided to cut my losses short and get out. This was a life lesson that was important to me. Knowing when it's time to let go. If I could go back in time, I would not change a thing because the real-life lessons I learned were priceless.

Opportunity can come in many ways. If you can keep an open mind and do some research before completely shutting something down, you'll be surprised at what you can gain. When that process happens, what can you say you've learned. There was no experience, no journey, some may even say it was luck. True opportunity is something you live through and can show people how it's possible to be replicated. That is why I strongly believe that your income is the biggest opportunity you have to becoming wealthy. I would often explain to individuals I presented to that if your house hold income monthly is $5,000 and all your expenses and debt amount to $3,500 that you are wealthy. Basically, you have $1,500 of disposable income to do as you wish. At the moment, I was explaining how having other people working for you can get you to this point, which is where all business people want to end up. It's called being able to make money while you are sleeping or residual income.

I then realized after the business failed that I could get to that point by looking into different financial opportunities. The best opportunity came to me when I went through the Dave Ramsey course at my church. I was initially skeptical about going to this class as well because I thought I had a good grasp on my finances. Dave's philosophy was to get out of debt, stay out of debt, let your income generate and build your wealth. This is when the proverbial light bulb shined bright in my head. I had been looking at this wrong. If I were out of debt and let my income build, I would be able to take on more opportunities.

If you are someone who is not good with money, or an immigrant in this country for the first time, my advice is don't get caught up with borrowing money. Americans borrow on everything. I remember growing up and having to use coins or dollar bills to pay for items in the vending machines and now they take credit cards.

Think about this, you are borrowing to pay for a soda and you are paying more. The soda cost $1.50 if you pay with cash, if you pay with a credit card they tack on $.15 cents, that brings your total to $1.65, then you are charged whatever APR your credit has at the end of the month. We live in a society that wants everything right now and we don't want to wait.

Now, in order to be profitable when it comes to opportunities you have to be somewhat knowledgeable. That comes with doing research. You just don't want to take on every opportunity that falls in your lap. The best thing to do is to do some research on the opportunity and make sure you understand it thoroughly. When I was doing MLM and I didn't understand something, I would make a note and ask the presenter at the end to explain this to me as if I were a child so I could better understand it.

There were a few chuckles sometimes but I needed clarification. I was told a story by my sister that a relative of ours emptied her 401k to buy investment properties. I can't sit here and tell you she made a bad decision because I don't know what opportunity showed up but I would never take money from a retirement account that's gaining compound interest to invest with. Again, I would suggest that with every opportunity that presents itself, research it and fully understand it to a degree that you are comfortable with before leaping into it.

# Chapter 7:

# Save For Retirement

Having goals are important in life. Goals help us to look forward to what is to come. Another great thing about goals are, you can track them. You can track your progress and that's why it's important to write them down. A goal that is not written down is a wish. If your goal is to buy a house in 5 years, write that goal down, acknowledge your savings plan, then come up with an action plan. You may need to get a second job to make enough income for the down payment. You may want to read up on the housing market in order to be more educated on your investment and you may need to do research on a realtor in the area that will help you meet your goals, all of these should be in your action plan plus whatever else you feel is important as stated in previous chapters.

One of the biggest goals that I believe all people should have but surprisingly many do not consider until it is to late is retirement. I recently read an article that stated that 68% of working Americans do not contribute to a 401k plan according to Forbes.com. Please do not fall victim to this statistic. If you work for a company that offers a 401k match, please contribute at least to the match percentage. If someone walked up to you and offered to give you free money legally, would you turn it down? I hope your answer is no.

One night while I was supervising at my part time job I decided to make small talk with one of the employees. His name was Oliver and he grew up in the projects of Hartford. I asked him how his weekend was and he responded it went well. He and his wife went to a R&B concert at the casino. He said that he enjoyed the experience and so did his wife.

We then turned our focus to football, talking about a player that was cut from the Giants and how his nine million dollar a year contract would be cut severely when he gets picked up from another team. Man, what I would do with nine million dollars I said. I then turned to him and asked what he would do with that amount of money. He said I wouldn't need nine million and he would be satisfied with just a million dollars. He would move down south where the cost of living is cheaper. He would buy a house with a man cave and design it the way he would like. He would set aside money for his kids and not allow them to touch it until they were 21 and after going through a financial course. He said he was putting money aside so that he can buy a house. He's never lived in a house before.

This was his dream, and as simple as it may seem, all he wanted was a place to call his own and to make sure that his family was taken care of. He didn't want to be rich or famous, he just wanted stability. I spoke to another older gentleman a couple months back. He has been retired from his main job for the past ten years. He started working at his current job soon after he retired from his main job. He didn't like working this job but he needed to because he owed on his house. He told me not to make the same mistake he had. He advised me if you are going to retire, make sure you retire debt free. Having debt and going into retirement is an equation for failure. If you implement what I have suggested in the earlier chapters, you will be in a great position when it comes to retirement.

# Chapter 8:

# Read More

I once read a story about an old man who lived on the same street as an elementary school. He spent most of his day on the porch outside enjoying the day. Every Wednesday was trash day, so he would put his trash out the following night. As systematic and unproblematic as this may seem, there was an issue. Every Wednesday when school would let out a group of kids would kick over his trash cans. The old man was a bit clever so he came up with an idea.

One Wednesday he called the kids over and told them that he would pay them one dollar every time they knocked over his trash cans. The little boys looked confused and replied to the old man, you want us to knock over your cans and you'll pay us a dollar said one of the boys, yes said the old man, we have an agreement said the boys. So, every Wednesday the boys would knock over the cans and then the old man would pay them a dollar.

The following Wednesday, the boys knocked over the trash cans and went to collect their dollar but the old man only gave them .75 cents. The boys were a little upset but hey they were still getting paid. The following week the boys knocked over the cans and went to collect their .75 cents and the old man gave them .50 cents. The boys were more upset that their payments were getting more and more reduced by the week but they still continued to do their job.

Finally, one Wednesday when the boys came to collect their fee, the old man told them that he could not pay them anymore. The boys were upset and told the old man that they weren't going to knock his cans over if he wasn't going to pay them, so the boys stopped. The moral of the story is, 'once you love doing something, don't let money corrupt it.'

A man once said, "The best way to hide something from Black people is to put it in a book". This statement rings true in many ways. We as a people have plenty of resources available to us but choose not to use them. The gold that we can dig out of a book or a well written article is priceless. Why do you think slave owners forbade teaching their slaves how to read and write? Information is power.

I remember growing up in Hartford Connecticut and going to my cousins house every Saturday. My cousin had three kids' younger than myself. She had two boys and a girl. I would always find myself playing video games for hours and hours with my younger male cousins. To get us to read a book was the equivalent of putting us on punishment. Hey, it was Saturday, we worked hard in school all week, and we deserved this break, that's what we told ourselves. Now their sister was a different story. She would lock herself in her room and she would read for hours. The family always raved about her love of reading. I never got into reading for leisure until much later in life. Fast forward, her love of reading excelled her in her academics. She excelled so much in her academics that she was top of her class in high school and received a full scholarship to college. The love of reading is a powerful tool. Studies have shown that children who read at a young age grow up to be very intelligent adults.

    A couple of my fraternity brothers and I decided to go to Dartmouth to visit a fraternity brother of ours. Once on the campus, he introduced us to some friends of his. One friend in particular I've kept in contact with off and on for years through social media outlets like Facebook and Instagram. She has become a very successful and powerful businesswoman. I remember a conversation I had with her one day. I was intrigued at how intelligent she was so I asked her how she became so smart. She told me that she came from a strict Haitian household. Her father did not want her to watch anything on television that didn't benefit her knowledge. She would watch the discovery channel, National Geographic, and Scientific programs. She would also read a lot of books. She said those two things molded her into the intellectual she is today.

The church I attend has a prison ministry. Every other weekend, the Pastor along with a few brothers from the church would go to a local prison and preach to some of the inmates. I remember signing up for this ministry and attending one of the sessions. It was very inspiring and fulfilling to know that we were reaching out to men who may have made wrong choices in their lives and introduced them to the Bible. I remember talking to one of the inmates there that recognized me from our elementary school days. We started up a conversation after the session was completed. I didn't ask him why he was there, because that would have been inappropriate but I did ask him what he did to pass the time. Surprisingly he said, reading. He said he does a lot of reading and it has made him more enlightened to many things he would not have known if not for being in his current circumstance.

I have read articles of prisoners finding clauses and loopholes in their cases because of all the reading they did of law books. I have read stories about prisoners obtaining their Master Degrees and law degrees in prison. Why can't we have that drive as free men and women to seek knowledge and better ourselves? Why does it take, in this cause, the lack of freedom to want to improve our love for reading? Reading is an essential key to unlocking vast doors in our pursuit of betterment.

I am glad that you have taken the time to read this book. It shows a commitment to better yourself. I hope you take some key points in this book and apply them to your everyday lives. If there's one thing to take away from this book, it's to read more. If you read about 10 minutes a day, you will be able to complete, on average, 12 books a year. I would like you to make a list of things that interest you, find books on the subject, and read them. That's what I did.

I wanted to get a better grip on my finances so I read Dave Ramsey's book "The Total Money Make Over" and George S. Clason "The Richest Man In Babylon". I wanted to learn more about business and real estate so I read Robert Kiyosaki's book "Rich Dad Poor Dad" and Gary Keller's book "The Millionaire Real Estate Investor". So, as you can see, reading about things that interest me is one of the most self-fulfilling feelings I can offer myself.

# Chapter 9:

# Look Out

While on your journey to building financial wealth, there are a few things you must watch out for. These things consist of predatory lending, payday loans, overdrafts, and Borrowing. While on my journey to financial freedom, these were a few things that reared its ugly head to try and deter me. If you were trapped in a hole, would you try and dig yourself out? I would suspect that you wouldn't. So, while you are trying to get out of debt and build wealth, try not to revert back to the behaviors that put you there in the first place. Knowing what to watch out for will help foster better results in shorter time.

**Predatory Lending:**

Predatory Lending is the practice of giving out loans with high interest rates for borrowers with bad or no credit history who do not qualify for the prime market. Predatory lending occurs when banks and mortgage providers target individuals with a lot of built up equity in their homes, talk them into refinancing and then give them higher interest to pay it off. These loans are absolutely terrible and they target lower income families. These lenders know that there's a sort of desperation for lower income families with bad credit to borrow money in order to get the things they need, so they rake up the interest rate on these loans and sell them. A recent study showed that lower income blacks received 2.4 times as many subprime loans than whites and upper income blacks receive 3 times as many subprime loans than whites.

Think about all the times you've listened to the radio and a car commercial comes on saying, "bad credit, no credit, forget it, we'll give you a loan". These lenders are preying on your desperation to get into a new vehicle. You probably have said to yourself, 'this is the best offer I can get', so you apply for this loan that has a high interest rate. When you do the math, you realize that you will pay half the loan amount or the entire amount in interest. For example, I remember the second car I purchased back in college. My first car was purchased for 500 dollars when I was in high school and lasted a very long time. While in college it started giving me problems so I decided I would look at a dealership to finance a car. I was on the verge of graduating and I had a job lined up so I was able to afford it. My mother and I went to the dealership in the area and I picked out the car I wanted. My mother didn't have the best of credit at the time so the sales associate told me I should put the loan in my name alone. When all the paper work was completed, I was so excited about my new vehicle that I didn't fully grasp the situation I put myself in. My loan broke down to this:

| Price of Vehicle | 12,000 |
|---|---|
| Life of the loan | 48 months |
| Monthly Payment | 370 |
| Interest Rate | 22% |
| Total Interest | 10,769.23 |
| Total Finance Amount | $22,769.23 |

As you can see from the chart above, my interest is almost half of the total price of the car. I learned from this experience. Every car that I have purchased after has been paid for in cash that I have saved up. I will not allow myself to ever have a car loan again.

**Payday Loans:**

Payday loans are one of the worst loans you can take out. A payday loan is a loan that has a very high interest rate and has to be paid back within a pay cycle or shortly after taking the loan out. It is basically a loan shark. The payday loan industry is a 9-billion-dollar industry. 1 in 20 households in the United States has taken one of these loans out.

A Pew Report found some common characteristics among pay day borrows:

1) **They are Africa Americans**
2) **They are renters**
3) **Do not have a four-year college degree**
4) **Are separated or divorced**
5) **Earn less than 40,000 a year**

Payday loans have extremely high interest rates because of the short-term cycle of the note. I have seen rates from 400%, 500%, 1000%, and even as high as 1500%. The way these loans work is by feeding off of the fact that most Americans do not have an emergency fund to cover a $400 emergency. That's where payday loans come into play. They give you a false sense of relief from an emergency. In order to take the loan out, you will need to pay a finance fee. Most people who take out these loans take out on average 8 loans. The sad thing about these loans are, you get so caught up in them and then behind that you end up having to ask family for money, take on extra hours at work, or even find another job to be able to pay the loan back. These are things that you should have done in the first place instead of taking the loan out. But we live in an instant gratification society where we always want things instantly.

Payday loans target lower income Americans. I read that there are more payday loans than both McDonalds and Starbucks combined in America. These businesses are set up close to military bases, in low income neighborhoods, and in African American communities. What makes it worse, is that they even hired a black celebrity to go on television promoting this product. I remember seeing a payday loan commercial with this particular celebrity on it several years back. Around this time, I was bad with money but I still had common sense. I called the number on the television screen and spoke to a representative who explained how the loan process went. She told me that the APR was around 800%. I did the math on my calculator for the amount of a $1000 loan and was shocked that someone would take out a loan like that. I told her that I was not going to take out the loan and asked her if people actually take out these loans, she replied confidently and said, "absolutely"!

Payday loans are never a good idea. A good way to stay away from these businesses, would be to have a small emergency fund saved up and doing the things that I have mentioned in the earlier chapters of this book. Another way to avoid these people is by doing your research. Always weigh your option when taking out any loans if you have to. Do the math, see if you can make the payments, if you can't, do not take out the loan.

**Overdraft Fees:**

An overdraft happens when you spend money from your bank account that you do not have. The average overdraft and ATM fee in the United states is around $35. The three largest banks in America earned more than $6 billion dollars on overdraft and ATM fees in 2015. How is this possible? Are we really this bad with money? I believe that we do have some common knowledge of money but once again we always need it now. When we want something, no matter the lack of money, we forgo all the red flags to get it. I was one who thought like this early on.

I remember being at work 8 years ago. I was one to never bring lunch with me. I would always purchase lunch. I would spend on average $10 a day, that's $50 a week, $200 a month. I spent $200 a month on lunch, that was quite excessive. One day I came to work and it was lunch time and I was hungry. I knew that I only had $5 in my checking account but I was determined to get my $10 lunch. I knew if I used the credit function on my debit card it would buy me 2 business days before it hit my account. I then proceeded to buy my lunch on credit. Obviously, I knew I wouldn't have the money to put in the bank in 2 days. So, I was charged a $35 overdraft fee. My $10 lunch cost me $45. All because I didn't pack a lunch.

These banks do well for themselves. They do so well that they have consumers lining up and begging them to borrow money that we've loaned to them. When we put our money in the bank, it is loaned out. The minimal interest that we earn is the bank giving us some form of payment for spending our money. When we mishandle money, we get burned and the banking institutions benefit greatly. Banks make enough money, so let's become money smart and start building our wealth and not theirs.

**Borrowing:**

As you can probably tell, the main focus of this section is to inform you of smarter ways to obtain money without having to ask or borrow. We live in a world where the turnaround is quick and easy and no one wants to work for it. People expect things done in the blink of an eye without really having to view the processes of how it was completed.

When you look deep into the root cause of our money issues, borrowing is at the root. We take out credit cards and get into financial trouble when we can't pay them back. We finance cars and get in financial trouble when we can't pay them back. We borrow to go to school and it causes us to be in some of the worst debt in our young adult lives. If we did not borrow but instead saved our money for the things we wanted, this country, our families, and our lives would be in far better shape.

Have you ever loaned a friend or a family member money before? Doesn't it change the dynamic of the relationship? Whenever you see that person you always have that thought in the back of your mind the debt that needs to be repaid. The person that owes you money will start avoiding you because they can't pay you back. This then causes tension in the relationship. When you consistently loan someone money, you are enabling bad habits. You wouldn't give an alcoholic a drink if they asked or a drug addict a hit. The same rule applies. We should not do this with loaning loved ones' money. If you have it, give it to them in love, under the condition they start to straighten out their financial life.

# Chapter 10:

# Pay It Forward

One of the most satisfying and gratifying things to me is helping others. Being influential in someone else's life, gives me a greater sense of purpose. Giving back can be in the form of donating money, time, or your knowledge. Areas you can donate to are: your local church, food banks, or to a scholarship program. You could volunteer your time to a multitude of events like cleanup efforts, local soup kitchens, or shelters. Ways you can donate your knowledge is by mentoring, being a big brother or big sister. There is a plethora of ways you can give back or pay it forward. I guarantee you will feel a sense of fulfillment once you do.

Do you know how important you are? Imagine the process it took to get you in this world. Imagine the journey that sperm took to get to the egg. Trillions of sperms died during this process and the one that had perseverance and strength was the one that created you. This entire process tells us that if you are in this world, you are extremely special because you faced unsurmountable odds. We shouldn't waste the precious time we have on this planet by questioning or doubting our true purpose. Each person will have a different purpose in life, and it is your responsibility to seek it out. Find those things in life that truly set you free and make you feel great.

I remember the first time I started tithing at the church I go to. I never really tithed before but I would give offerings from time to time. I never understood why I should give 10% of my paycheck, so I didn't. When I started getting my financial life in order and the course that introduced me to a lot of pertinent information was in church, I decided to start tithing. Something amazing started to happen once I gave. That year was one of the best financial years of my career. I made a lot of money and received a lot of recognition that year. I believe that I was rewarded for tithing.

Sometimes paying it forward means letting go. You are probably thinking what I mean by this. Well, let's look at a situation that happened to my wife and I. We started the process of getting our finances together because we wanted to buy a house. At the time, my wife was pregnant and we were expecting our child shortly. We lived in a two-bedroom apartment on the second floor. I thought, if this child was anything like our first child, we would either need to move to an apartment on the first floor or buy a house because we would have noise complaints every day. My child did not believe in walking or not jumping on furniture. After a mutual decision, we decided to purchase a house with 3 bedrooms and a lot of backyard space for the kids to run till their hearts content.

In the process of buying a home and trying to control our debt we started to pay off our credit cards. There was one particular card that was hard for me to pay off. It was a card that my wife opened and gave to her cousin to use. The balance on the card was around $1,500. I told my wife to handle the conversation with her relative about paying the card off. My wife told me that her relative agreed to pay the card off with a bonus she would be getting from work.

A few weeks passed and the card wasn't paid off so I brought the topic back up to my wife. I asked her if she had heard any updates from her relative, she responded that she had not. I asked her to follow up with the relative. She came back and told me that the relative had received the bonus check but it wasn't what she had hoped for and couldn't pay us back. We decided we would put her on a repayment plan so that we could start receiving some of the money back. That plan lasted about a month. At this point I was upset and disappointed with the relative. I felt that she betrayed us.

One day my wife and I sat down to organize our debt. We had received a big bonus check from work and decided we would put it all on our debt to cancel a few out. We decided to pay the card off that the relative owed money on. We decided to do this under one condition. It was that we would not ask the relative to pay us back, that we would clear her of the debt. We knew she wasn't being malicious or greedy by not paying us but that she like a lot of people, just didn't have the money. We valued the relationship and family atmosphere that we all had. In actuality, when we looked deeper into the situation it was more our fault than hers.

Once we forgave the debt, the atmosphere around family gatherings changed. There wasn't any awkwardness towards one another. Both parties felt like a burden had been lifted. We now realize that if we give someone money, it is better to do so as a gift and not a loan. We hope that our experience will teach the relative to do the same and forgive someone of something they may have done or to forgive a debt. Pay it forward.

# Chapter 11:

# Closing

I believe that life is too short to worry about insignificant things that won't bring true happiness. Money is an object, a tool to be used in order to obtain what you feel is the ideal life. Like any tool, one needs to learn how to properly handle it, know the safety procedures, and how to achieve full potential of the tool. If you want to build a house, you would need to use a hammer and not an eating utensil. Using the wrong tool or improper use of a tool can lead to failure. The same goes with money. This is why I don't understand why personal finance courses aren't taught in every middle school, high school, and college curriculum across the country. Learning these practical skills would benefit each of us and save us from being irresponsible adults that lack the responsibility to gain and maintain financial security.

There was a video that I saw on the internet with a young man singing about not being prepared by the educational system for the real world. He sung about not knowing how to do taxes, financial advices, how to trade stocks, the history of money, or how to do a budget. As an adult looking back at what he was saying, I find myself slightly afraid for the next generation. We are living in a country that our government is in debt and does not know how to balance proper finances. As a parent, I would love for the school system to teach my children personal finance but I know that won't happen so it is my responsibility to teach my children and not rely on the educational system.

I hope that the information provided in this book proves to be uplifting and beneficial. I want you to be able to break the generational curse of handling money poorly. I would like for you to become financially self-sufficient and to be able to leave an inheritance for your children and your children's children. Leaving an inheritance can go further than just money. It is the knowledge that you will bestow on your children, that's priceless.

There is an Old English Proverb that goes, "Give a man a fish, he eats for a day, teach a man to fish and he will eat for a lifetime." This proverbs states that if you do something for someone without showing them how you've done it, they will never be self-sufficient.

My faith lives in God. I attend church and as stated before in a previous chapter, I tithe. I have read the Bible from beginning to end and I research scriptures that my Pastor preaches on. When reading the Bible, you notice that the topic of money comes up a lot. I believe that Jesus knew that what men held close to their heart is where their faith would lie. This is one of the reasons I believe that money is brought up so much.

Jesus tries to warn us about how addictive money can become and to not put our faith in it. Learning about money, using it as a tool, and allowing it to work for you is sound advice. Conquer money and don't allow it to conquer you. Follow the advice and you can't go wrong. Be blessed.

For more resources and updates on events, please follow me on IG @Reidestatellc, Facebook Reid Estate For The Mind LLC, and visit my website www.reidestate.co

# Citation Page

"Big Banks Rack up $6.4 Billion in ATM and Overdraft Fees ..." Web. 19 Apr. 2017.

"Mortgage Calculator." Web. 19 Apr. 2017.

"Mortgage Payment Calculator | TD Canada Trust." Web. 19 Apr. 2017.

"The Case for Reparations by Ta-Nehisi Coates - The Atlantic." Web. 19 Apr. 2017.

"The Retirement Crisis: Why 68% Of Americans Aren't Saving ..." Web. 19 Apr. 2017.

"The Truth Behind '40 Acres and a Mule' | African American ..." Web. 19 Apr. 2017.

Clason, George S. *The Richest Man in Babylon: Now Revised and Updated for the 21st Century*. United States: BN Pub., 2007. Print.

Kiyosaki, Robert T. *Rich Dad Poor Dad: What the Rich Teach Their Kids About Money That the Poor and Middle Class Do Not!* Perseus Distribution Services, 2017. Print.

Ramsey, Dave. *The Total Money Makeover: A Proven Plan for Financial Fitness*. Nashville, TN: Nelson , an Imprint of Thomas Nelson, 2013. Print.